CW00321885

5 A DAY TO KEEP YOU Joyful

5 A DAY TO KEEP YOU JOYFUL

Copyright © Rachel and Andrew Sainsbury, 2018

All rights reserved.

No part of this book may be reproduced by any means, nor transmitted, nor translated into a machine language, without the written permission of the publishers.

Rachel and Andrew Sainsbury have asserted their right to be identified as the authors of this work in accordance with sections 77 and 78 of the Copyright, Designs and Patents Act 1988.

Condition of Sale
This book is sold subject to the condition that it shall not, by way of trade or otherwise, be lent, resold, hired out or otherwise circulated in any form of binding or cover other than that in which it is published and without a similar condition including this condition being imposed on the subsequent purchaser.

An Hachette UK Company
www.hachette.co.uk

Summersdale Publishers Ltd
Part of Octopus Publishing Group Limited
Carmelite House
50 Victoria Embankment
LONDON
EC4Y 0DZ
UK

www.summersdale.com

Printed and bound in the Czech Republic

ISBN: 978-1-78685-225-0

Substantial discounts on bulk quantities of Summersdale books are available to corporations, professional associations and other organisations. For details contact general enquiries: telephone: +44 (0) 1243 771107 or email: enquiries@summersdale.com.

5 A DAY TO KEEP YOU *Joyful*

DAILY INSPIRATION FOR A HEALTHY, HAPPY MIND

Rachel & Andrew Sainsbury

summersdale

To..

Message...

....

....

....

....

....

From..

Everyone knows it's good to eat five portions of fruit and veggies a day to keep your body healthy, but what about a five-a-day for your mind?

Read one page a day from each of the five chapters for a more joyful you.

ENJOY!

HERE ARE YOUR FIVE CHAPTERS:

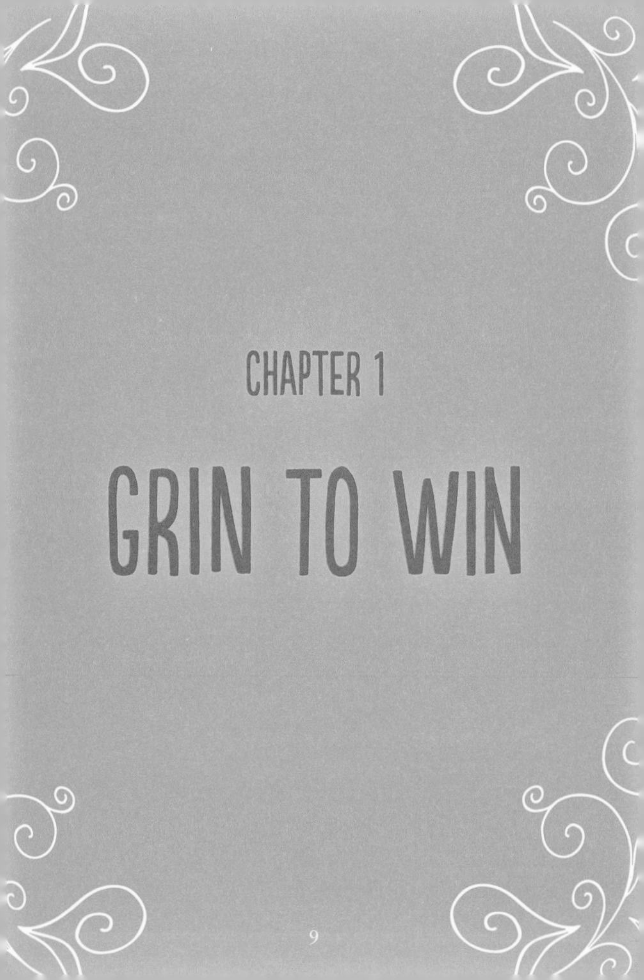

CHAPTER 1

GRIN TO WIN

HERE'S WHY YOU SHOULD GRIN TO WIN

One smile can be as stimulating to the brain as consuming 2,000 chocolate bars. So if you fancy a happiness boost, just put on a big cheesy grin (as wide as possible, please). And because smiling is contagious, you'll make others feel good too.

A smile costs
nothing,
but gives much.
It enriches
those who receive,
without making poorer
those who
give.

Rabbi Samson Raphael Hirsch

HANG OUT WITH HAPPY

A good way to achieve what you want in life is to mix with those who already have it. So spend time with people who are happy and optimistic and you'll soon feel happy and optimistic too.

LOOKIN' GOOOOOOOD!

The sexiest curve on your body is your smile. Flaunt it! What's more, it takes half as many muscles to smile as to frown. So looking good has never been so easy.

CAPTURE SMILES

Capture moments of real happiness with a photograph and display them around your house or workplace. Looking at them will instantly recall these moments in your mind and conjure up a smile in the here and now, bringing new smiles to life.

A SMILE IS HAPPINESS YOU'LL FIND RIGHT UNDER YOUR NOSE.

Tom Wilson

PUT A SMILE ON YOUR FACE

Even if you're feeling grumpy, put a smile on your face and happiness will follow. This is because the relationship between emotion and behaviour is a two-way street: behaviour (smiling) can cause emotion (happiness).

EVERYONE UNDERSTANDS A SMILE

Smiling is universal – members of tribes completely disconnected from the outside world use smiling to convey the same meaning as we do. So wherever you are in the world, wear a smile.

A smile will almost always be reciprocated with a smile. By sharing one smile with another person, we're actually creating and sending many more smiles out into the world.

SMILE WHEN YOU'RE TIRED

The next time you're feeling lethargic, put a smile on your face. It will give you a natural energy boost and is healthier than buying an energy drink!

Sometimes your joy
is the source of your smile,
but sometimes your smile
can be the source of
your joy.

Thích Nhất Hạnh

Happiness goes toward the ones who know how to laugh.

Japanese proverb

SMILING IS GOOD FOR BUSINESS

Smiling waiters and waitresses make more money from tips. Smiling entrepreneurs are more likely to attract investment. So smile; it's good for your bank balance too.

BE MORE CHILDLIKE

Children smile as many as 400 times a day, while adults only average around 15 times a day. Children are highly aware of their environment, living every moment to the full – make an effort to do the same and smile more.

Every smile
makes you
a day
younger.

Chinese proverb

ACCESSORISE WITH A SMILE

It's been scientifically proven that we are physically more attractive to others when we smile – so a smile is a very inexpensive way to improve your looks!

SMILE LIST

Write a list of five things that make you smile, such as an old couple holding hands or a child playing in the rain, and look out for them throughout your day to bring on that happy feeling.

SMILE TO RELAX

Your simplest facial expression – a smile – happens when your muscles relax, which instantly makes you feel both emotionally and physically good.

THE MAN WORTHWHILE IS THE ONE WHO WILL SMILE WHEN EVERYTHING GOES DEAD WRONG.

Ella Wheeler Wilcox

CALM WITH A SMILE

Smiling is the most reliable way to get an anxious person to relax, and in turn reduce your own anxiety.

BE POSITIVE AND LIVE LONGER

Most people assume that positive thinking is just something we do to help us achieve our goals, but in fact, a positive attitude can add years to your life.

SMILE AND THE WHOLE WORLD SMILES WITH YOU

Smiling is such a simple act of kindness, and the powerful 'ripples' smiling creates are impossible to measure.

ROMANCE WITH A SMILE

Couples who smile together tend to stay together and report higher satisfaction in their relationships.

Dalai Lama

TURN A WORRY INTO A FUNNY ANECDOTE

Have you noticed how today's worries turn into tomorrow's funny stories? More often than not, today's problems become less of an issue over time. Imagine yourself at a point in the future looking back, smiling and laughing at today's worries – you will realise they're not so bad after all.

SMILES ARE EVERYWHERE

Find smiles everywhere, even in everyday objects – like buildings or in the froth of your latte. It will make you aware of your own positivity.

SMILE FOR GOOD HEALTH

The health benefits of smiling include increasing mood-enhancing hormones (such as endorphins and oxytocin), reducing stress-inducing hormones (such as cortisol) and lowering blood pressure.

ALWAYS LAUGH WHEN YOU CAN. IT IS CHEAP MEDICINE.

Lord Byron

SMILE AND FEEL RICH

In one study, it took a cash gift of up to £16,000 to generate the same level of brain stimulation as one smile! On this basis, if you smiled 62.5 times a day (about once every 15 minutes over 16 hours), you would feel like a millionaire every day!

CHAPTER 2

DO GOOD, FEEL GOOD

HERE'S WHY YOU SHOULD DO GOOD, FEEL GOOD

Doing good, by showing kindness to a friend, or helping out a colleague or a neighbour triggers the brain's reward circuitry. This causes the release of fabulous 'feel good' endorphins into the brain, reducing stress and making you feel gooooood.

When I do good, I feel good. When I do bad, I feel bad. That's my religion.

Abraham Lincoln, on a saying he heard at a church meeting in Indiana

GIVE MORE THAN YOU TAKE

The more we care for others, the greater our own sense of well-being. Think about the happiest people you know – do they give more than they take, or take more than they give?

FILL YOUR HEART AS WELL AS YOUR HEAD

We place great importance on filling our brains with knowledge. We should put as much care into filling our hearts with compassion.

GIVE A COMPLIMENT

Because everyone loves one.

The meaning of life
is to
find your gift.
The purpose of life
is to
give it away.

Anonymous

WE CAN FIND COMMON GROUND ONLY BY MOVING TO HIGHER GROUND.

Jim Wallis

BE KIND IN THE MIDDLE

At the beginning and end of our lives we are so dependent on the kindness of others. Don't forget to be kind towards others in the middle.

GIVE A GIFT

Giving the smallest of gifts can result in a surprisingly long-lasting change in happiness for the giver. A thoughtful, homemade or inexpensive gift could be one of the best investments you ever make.

DOUBLE WHAMMY

Because selfless acts make you feel happy, any act of altruism is its own reward. In addition, the memories of your act of kindness can induce positive feelings time and time again.

We make a living
by what we get,
but we make a life by
what we give.

Anonymous

The best way to cheer yourself up is to try to cheer somebody else up.

Mark Twain

HELPER'S HIGH

Try putting others first more often. By volunteering, lending a helping hand or just doing small acts of kindness for people, you will get a 'helper's high' in return and become happier.

The world is changed by your example, not by your opinion.

Paulo Coelho

ONE PERSON CAN MAKE A BIG CHANGE

Even if only one individual creates peace and happiness within themselves, they can send positive ripples throughout their home, workplace or local community.

IT'S BETTER TO GIVE THAN TO RECEIVE

Ask people whether they will be happier after spending money on themselves or others and most people will tick the 'me' box. However, research shows that the exact opposite is true – people become much happier when buying for loved ones rather than themselves.

GOOD FOR THE BRAIN

Neuroscientists have demonstrated that helping others activates the same areas of the brain as those involved in the pleasure responses of eating and being in love. One study even found the same was true when participants just thought about helping others.

BE KIND WHENEVER POSSIBLE. IT IS ALWAYS POSSIBLE.

Dalai Lama

A superior man is modest in his speech, but exceeds in his actions

Confucius

PURE MOTIVATION

Once you have pure and sincere motivation, all the rest follows.

THE THOUGHT
MANIFESTS AS THE
WORD; THE WORD
MANIFESTS AS THE DEED;
THE DEED DEVELOPS
INTO HABIT; AND THE
HABIT HARDENS
INTO CHARACTER.

Anonymous

Do unto others as you would have them do unto you.

Luke 6:31

LOVE EACH OTHER

Humans are social creatures. Caring for each other is the basis of our life together.

All that is
not given
is lost.

Indian proverb

BE MAGNANIMOUS

Magnanimous people have no jealousy or vanity. They rejoice in others' success and support those who are suffering. Be magnanimous, and you'll find you are the one who feels the most uplifted.

HAPPINESS IS THE ONLY GOOD. THE TIME TO BE HAPPY IS NOW. THE PLACE TO BE HAPPY IS HERE. THE WAY TO BE HAPPY IS TO MAKE OTHERS SO.

Robert Green Ingersoll

The time is always right
to do what is right.

Martin Luther King Jr

IMPRESS YOURSELF

Don't live your life impressing others.
Live your life impressing yourself.

STRENGTH FROM VIRTUE

The display of strength by one person does not diminish the strength of others – quite the opposite in fact. Onlookers are elevated and inspired by observing the virtuous actions of others.

CHAPTER 3

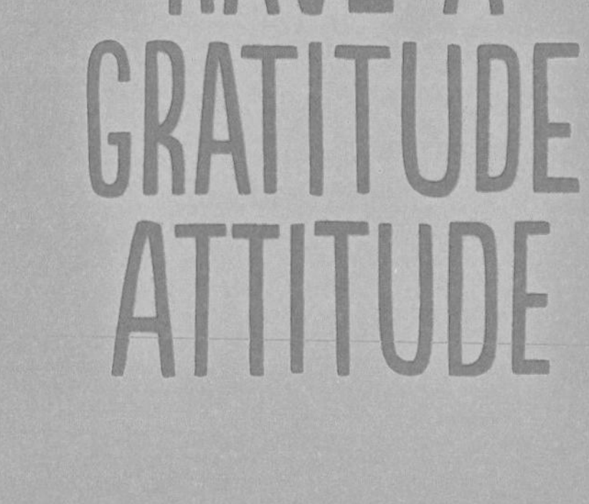

HAVE A GRATITUDE ATTITUDE

HERE'S WHY YOU SHOULD HAVE A GRATITUDE ATTITUDE

Not appreciating happy events and dwelling on problems isn't good for your well-being, but being grateful can magnify good memories and make you happier. Here's a simple, proven way to develop a gratitude attitude. Before you snuggle down each night, ask yourself, what three things am I most grateful for today?

The happiest people don't have the best of everything; they just make the best of everything.

Anonymous

CONCENTRATE ON THE GOOD

Pessimistic people get the same opportunities as optimistic people, but pessimistic people tend to overlook this. If you see things negatively, chances are you'll end up feeling unhappy. But if you look for the positive, you're much more likely to have a happier outlook.

YOU ARE PERFECTLY IMPERFECT

Some psychologists believe depression arises when a person compares themselves to others. We feel good when we measure up well, when we conform to or exceed the norm, but we tend to feel bad when we do not. Accept that you are unique and the pressure to conform will vanish.

CELEBRATE YOUR BIRTHDAY

When your birthday comes, you have a choice. You can moan about getting older or you can celebrate the miraculous achievement that your life has been to date. If there's one thing to celebrate, it's the achievement of being alive.

Feeling **gratitude** *and not* **expressing** *it, is like wrapping a* **present** *and* **not giving it.**

William Arthur Ward

WELCOME MISHAPS

As the saying goes, the person who makes no mistakes, makes nothing. Mistakes are simply reminders that life is a creative process and what lies ahead is enhanced by what has preceded it.

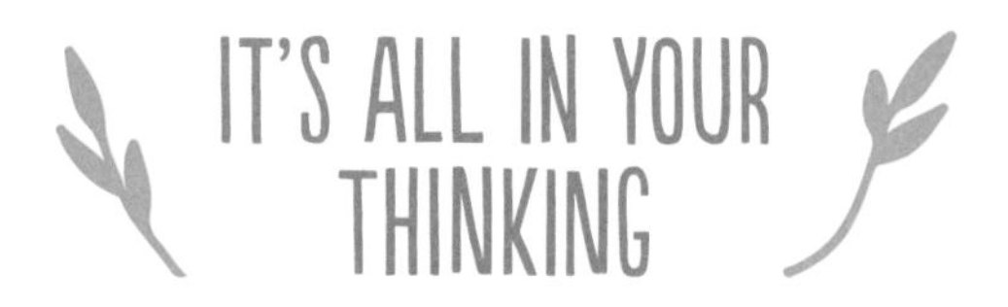

IT'S ALL IN YOUR THINKING

Very little is needed to create a happy life. It is all contained in your way of thinking. Happiness and contentedness all depend on the content of your thoughts.

IT'S GETTING BETTER

The media peddle bad news because they think bad news is more interesting than good. This can skew our perceptions of the world towards negativity, making us believe the world is being stripped of goodness, when the opposite is true. Globally speaking, life is getting better all the time – the average person is healthier, has more financial freedom and better access to education.

FOLKS ARE USUALLY ABOUT AS HAPPY AS THEY MAKE UP THEIR MINDS TO BE.

Abraham Lincoln

RETRAIN YOUR BRAIN

The difference between being a slave to a habit and being in positive control of your life is nothing more than the operation of tiny electrical circuits in your brain. Choose to change your perspective and you'll change these circuits. It just takes a little time and practice.

Become a possibilitarian. No matter how dark things seem to be or actually are, raise your sights and see possibilities – always see them, for they're always there.

Norman Vincent Peale

A SETBACK IS AN OPPORTUNITY TO START AGAIN MORE INTELLIGENTLY.

Henry Ford

TIME TO FIND HAPPINESS

It's a great time to be alive – you have more time than ever to find happiness and meaning in your life.

Era	Life expectancy
Neolithic	20 years
Bronze Age	26 years
Medieval	30 years
Today	80 years+

One joy dispels a hundred cares.

Confucius

LOOK FOR GOOD

Search for the good and go out of your way to find it. Your reality will change for the better.

DECIDE TO BE HAPPY

Make up your mind to be happy and appreciate what you have. Your future has as much to offer you as you make up your mind to allow it to have.

Be content with what you have, rejoice in the way things are. When you realise there is nothing lacking, the whole world belongs to you.

Lao Tzu

BE GRATEFUL FOR EVERYONE

A wise person knows that
there is something to be
learned from everyone.

HAPPINESS IS FOUND IN WHAT YOU ALREADY HAVE

If striving after material objects really brought about permanent happiness, then those with wealth would all have lasting happiness.

THE MORE WE ARE AWARE OF WHAT TO BE GRATEFUL FOR, THE HAPPIER WE BECOME.

Ezra Taft Benson

TAKE THE ROUGH WITH THE SMOOTH

Without mud, there would be no flowers.

THANK YOUR EFFORT

Effort brings its own reward. If you work hard, you will feel a greater level of satisfaction from what you do. Be satisfied with a job well done, even if no one seems to notice.

CHOOSE TO BE GLAD

Aim to find some aspect – no matter how small – in every situation that you are glad about. Playing this game sometimes requires a bit of imagination, but the outcome is always the same – you'll feel better and more positive than before.

The real gift of gratitude is that the more grateful you are, the more present you become.

Robert Holden

Happiness isn't about getting what you want all the time. It's about loving what you have.

Asher Roth

SUN WORSHIP

The sun provides us with light, warmth and energy to enable us to live and thrive.

Watch a sunrise and be grateful for its gifts.

QUESTION NEGATIVE THOUGHTS

If a negative thought comes your way, dispute it. Question if it is really true. You may be surprised to learn that very often it isn't.

REMEMBER A KISS

Recall a moment when you kissed someone on impulse and realised that that someone loved you as much as you loved them.

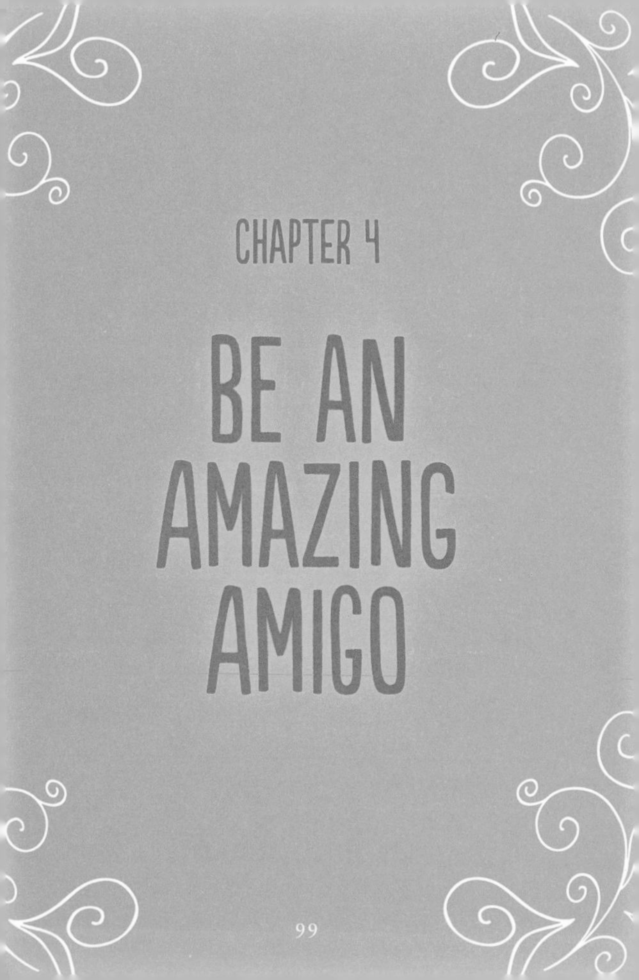

CHAPTER 4

BE AN AMAZING AMIGO

HERE'S WHY YOU SHOULD BE AN AMAZING AMIGO

Relationships are one of the most important contributors to happiness. Close relationships with family and friends provide meaning and increase our feelings of self-worth. Creating new connections and strengthening current ones are essential for your happiness.

A friend
is someone who
gives you total
freedom
to be yourself.

Jim Morrison

PEOPLE WILL
FORGET WHAT YOU
SAID, PEOPLE WILL
FORGET WHAT YOU DID,
BUT PEOPLE WILL NEVER
FORGET HOW YOU MADE
THEM FEEL.

Maya Angelou

WHAT'S IMPORTANT?

The most common deathbed regrets relate to neglected relationships, not unfinished work.

INVEST IN PEOPLE

Research shows that people who win the lottery usually find themselves at the same level of happiness they had before their big win after only a few months. In contrast to material things, however, people continue to derive happiness from relationships for much, much longer.

So invest in people and not just things for a happier you!

BUY EXPERIENCES

Studies show that the best way to spend money, in terms of the happiness it brings you, is to buy experiences, not material goods. Go out for a meal with a friend, go on holiday, go to a gig, in fact get involved in anything that provides an opportunity to do things with others – it's experiences that represent better value for money.

Walking with a friend in the dark is better than walking alone in the light.

Helen Keller

YOU ARE NOT ALONE

One of the main causes of unhappiness is the feeling of isolation. Recognise that you are not alone – there are countless people out there who would be grateful for your company.

THE SUPPORT OF FRIENDS

Can you think of anything that inspires you and keeps you positive as much as the support of friends? Sometimes, friends need inspiring too.

HUG MORE

Regular hugs and the human touch not only increase feelings of contentedness in life, but improve health and extend life – for both the giver and the receiver. There is no shortage of people you know who would love a hug right now.

A FRIEND IS A GIFT YOU GIVE YOURSELF.

Robert Louis Stevenson

BEST FRIEND

What's the best thing to be best at? Having the best house, best car, best TV or other material goods? Or being the best friend?

REAL FRIENDSHIP

Friends through money and power are not real friends. The best way to create friends is through a warm heart.

OUR RELATIONSHIPS MAKE US

Neuroscientists are discovering that relationships actually structure our brains. It is not our brains that make our relationships, but rather our relationships that make our brains. We are not individual, autonomous beings; we are the product of our relationships.

A friend is one who knows you and loves you just the same.

Elbert Hubbard

We are each of us
angels
with only one wing;
and we can only
fly
by embracing
one another.

Luciano De Crescenzo

CHERISH EACH OTHER

When we cherish others, both ourselves and others become happy. If we cherish ourselves more than others, unhappiness occurs, both for ourselves and others.

LIVING IN HARMONY

To live peacefully, we must trust those we depend on, and care for those who depend on us.

LOVE IS THE ABILITY AND WILLINGNESS TO ALLOW THOSE THAT YOU CARE FOR TO BE WHAT THEY CHOOSE FOR THEMSELVES.

Wayne Dyer

GOOD FROM CARING

Most of the good that comes out of the world is from the caring of others.

FOOD FOR WELL-BEING

Friends are the food that nourishes your emotional well-being.

Friendship is
born at that moment
when one person says to
another: 'What! You too?
I thought I was the
only one!'

C. S. Lewis

CARE FOR OTHERS

Numerous studies show that the happiest people are those who shift the focus away from themselves and toward the needs of others.

He who sows courtesy reaps friendship, and he who plants kindness gathers love.

Saint Basil of Caesarea

HUMANS ARE SOCIAL CREATURES

From the study of prisoners in solitary confinement, it has been proven that people deprived of human contact have reduced social and mental functioning. Humans are social creatures; it is important to spend time with your fellow humans.

Grief can
take care of itself,
but to get the full value
of **joy** you
must have
somebody
to **divide it with.**

Mark Twain

OKAY, WE ARE
DIFFERENT IT'S TRUE.
AND I DON'T LIKE TO DO
ALL THE THINGS THAT YOU
DO. BUT HERE'S ONE THING
TO THINK THROUGH, YOU'RE
A LOT LIKE ME AND I'M
A LOT LIKE YOU!

Robert Alan Silverstein

TREAT EVERYONE LIKE A FRIEND

Treat everyone like they are a good friend – you will find that warmth and kindness flows more easily.

WHO DO YOU ADMIRE?

Tell at least one person everyday something you like, admire or appreciate about them.

CHAPTER 5

LIVE IN THE NOW

HERE'S WHY YOU SHOULD LIVE IN THE NOW

When you don't worry about the future, and don't have regrets about the past, you exist purely in the moment. Enjoy the moment – it's where happiness is found.

*Breathe. Let go.
And remind yourself
that this very moment
is the only one you know
you have for sure.*

Oprah Winfrey

HAPPINESS IS A WAY OF TRAVEL – NOT A DESTINATION.

Roy Goodman

WATCH YOUR THOUGHTS

Most stresses and anxieties are the result of what happens in your head, not what happens to your body. Take comfort in knowing that most of your negative thoughts never actually become reality.

MAKE IT A FIRST-TIME EXPERIENCE

Try this simple exercise to reveal the wonders of life. For every sound you hear, every sight you see, every flavour you taste, imagine you are experiencing it for the very first time. You can't help but feel some wonder in life's simple pleasures.

MAKE EVERY NOTE COUNT

Some of the world's greatest musicians say they play each performance as if it were their last. When musicians play with passion, the difference is profound. Imagine the result if you played every performance of your life in this way and how much more enjoyable and fulfilling it would be.

Feelings come and go like clouds in a windy sky. Conscious breathing is my anchor.

Thích Nhất Hạnh

IMMERSE YOURSELF

High levels of happiness can occur when we're immersed in engrossing activities. Losing yourself on the dance floor, playing the banjo, surfing a wave or painting a picture can make you feel energised. Do things that absorb you and help you live in the moment – it will leave you feeling alive and uplifted.

BREATHE

When we concentrate on our breathing – when we really hear it coming and going – peace comes.

If not now,
when?
If not you,
who?

Hillel the Elder

LET GO

It's normal to feel happy about good fortune, sad about bad events and annoyed at the behaviour of others, but once you have acknowledged your feelings, let them go.

NOTHING IS PERMANENT IN THIS WICKED WORLD, NOT EVEN OUR TROUBLES.

Anonymous

SERENITY FROM ACCEPTANCE

Serenity comes naturally from acceptance, especially of the things you cannot change.

MEDITATE

An MRI scan of the academic-turned-Buddhist monk, Matthieu Ricard aka 'The World's Happiest Man', showed that he and other long-term meditators have vastly increased activity in the left prefrontal cortex. Activity in this part of the brain is key to our happiness so get meditating for a mood boost.

Realise deeply that the present moment is all you will ever have.

Eckhart Tolle

MEDITATION IN A NUTSHELL

Concentrate on a movement, a sound, an image, without strain. If your attention wanders, gently bring your attention back without concern. Before you know it, you'll be meditating.

RELAX

When you try to control absolutely everything, enjoyment is reduced. Sometimes you just need to relax, breathe, let go, and live in the moment.

Every morning, we are born again. What we do today is what matters most.

Jack Kornfield

BE PRESENT LIKE A CHILD

Children instinctively live in the present moment. Just observe a young child to see how it's done.

SLOW IT DOWN

When you are relaxed, your breathing slows. By consciously slowing down your breathing you will relax quickly.

I would love to live
like a river flows,
carried by
the surprise
of its own
unfolding.

John O'Donohue

WEAR SUPERMAN SOCKS

Remind yourself of how present and uninhibited you were as a child by wearing funny socks or silly underpants for the day.

TODAY'S PEACE

Worrying does not take away tomorrow's troubles; it takes away today's peace.

LEARN TO BE MINDFUL

We spend up to 50 per cent of our time caught up in our thoughts. Excessive mind wandering about the past or planning for the future can lead to unhappiness, so being mindful – engaging in the here and now – allows us to live with greater clarity and peace of mind.

IF YOU WANT
TO CONQUER
THE ANXIETY OF
LIFE, LIVE IN THE
MOMENT, LIVE IN
THE BREATH.

Amit Ray

MINDFULNESS IN A NUTSHELL

Mindfulness is the practice of bringing all your awareness to the here and now. You don't need to try to clear your mind of all thoughts and feelings, instead, try to take a backseat to them and witness them as they come and go.

Wherever you are,
be all there.

Jim Elliot

LIST YOUR JOYFUL NOTES AND IDEAS HERE

....

....

....

....

....

....

....

....

....

....

....